Neurons ADHD

Marielle Bayliss

Illustrations by Kellyanne Thorne

GRAFFEG

Hi, I'm Fizz, and I'm a neuron!

Let me explain what neurons are...

4

What is a neuron?

Neurons are important for everything your body does.

Got an itch?
We'll help you scratch!

Bored? We'll get you daydreaming.

Nothing happens without neurons knowing about it!

From Brrrrrr to Brain!

We neurons pick up on feelings,
like temperature, then send
messages to the brain.

10

The brain then sends a command
to the body to tell it what to do.

Excellent idea!
Shivering warms the body.

Though I don't like the look of those crusty jumpers.

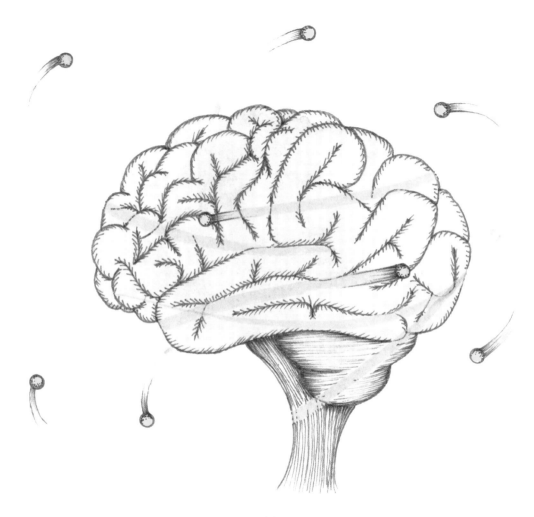

Your brain is in charge of
everything your body does.
It makes decisions based on
the messages we send.

As you can see...

...things happen...

...quickly around here.

Even queues!

Let's zoom down the spinal cord! This is the main way neurons travel.

Queue
Here

Would the brain
like a scarf?

Does the brain like jokes?

23

Am I asking too many questions?

It's good to ask questions... and wait for answers. People's brains can be wired differently; some people deal with one job at a time and finish it before moving on.

25

Some people are excited to try new things immediately and do lots of jobs at once.

And others like to fully understand new things first.

Neuron Pathways

Inside your brain there are lots of networks of neurons, like roads. Neurons pass information along these roads. It's a bit like playing catch the ball, but with messages.

If someone has ADHD, the neurons might have trouble catching some of the balls, so information takes longer to come through.

29

This means that it takes the brain more time to switch off, even when tired.

Or concentrate on one task at a time.

Mei has ADHD.

ADHD

ADHD stands for Attention Deficit Hyperactivity Disorder, but it doesn't have to be thought of as a lack of attention or a disorder. For people with ADHD, the brain works a little differently. It can affect how they act, their emotions and their concentration.

Sometimes, ADHD can be helpful. In fact, people with ADHD might notice things that others miss.

But sometimes it isn't.

ADHD is different for each person. People might:

- Start jobs without finishing them.
- Not like waiting around.
- Ask lots of questions.
- Not like planning.
- Act without thinking.
- Not like waiting for their turn.
- Avoid organising their things.
- Find it hard to unwind.

But there are also ways that
ADHD can help. People might:
- Dive into new situations.
- Take on several tasks at once.
- Make friends easily.
- Be super focused.
- Finish tasks quickly when focused.
- Be passionate about their hobbies.
- Notice things that others miss.
- Ask lots of questions.

ADHD can feel like bubbles of excitement in your head that have to pop. Sometimes, popping them is great fun.

But sometimes it's too much.

These fizzing bubbles can cause frustration, or make people feel anxious or restless.

It can be tempting to dive right into things, but sometimes it's very useful to plan!

Mei's Action Plan:

- Aim for reachable goals.
- Set simpler tasks and steps to follow.
- If I don't finish a task, I can complete it later.
- Be proud of myself when I finish tasks.
- Be kind to myself — I can't do everything.

- Stay healthy with regular meals, water and plenty of sleep.

- Take restful breaks.

- Recognise when I'm becoming anxious.

- Use ADHD strengths when learning or playing.

- Change goals and routines regularly so they don't become boring.

Embrace being you!

ADHD is like a pattern —
it's the way some brains work
and NOT a disorder.

We all have unique brains and do
things in our own way.

Neurons and ADHD
Published in Great Britain in 2025 by Graffeg Limited.
ISBN 9781802587869

Graffeg Limited, 15 Neptune Court, Vanguard Way,
Cardiff, CF24 5PJ, Wales, UK. Tel: 01554 824000.
croeso@graffeg.com. www.graffeg.com

Marielle Bayliss is hereby identified as the author of this
work in accordance with section 77 of the Copyright,
Designs and Patents Act 1988.

Printed by FINIDR, s.r.o., Czechia.

A CIP Catalogue record for this book is available from the
British Library.

This book is designed for children, printed with materials
and processes that are safe and meet all applicable
European safety requirements. The book does not contain
elements that could pose health or safety risks under
normal and intended use.

We hereby declare that this product complies with all
applicable requirements of the General Product Safety
Regulation (GPSR) and any other relevant EU legislation.

Appointed EU Representative:
Easy Access System Europe Oü, 16879218
Mustamäe tee 50, 10621, Tallinn, Estonia
gpsr.requests@easproject.com

The publisher gratefully acknowledges the financial
support of this book by the Books Council of Wales.
www.gwales.com.

1 2 3 4 5 6 7 8 9

Book Series

Neurons and Epilepsy
ISBN 9781802587821

Neurons and Autism
ISBN 9781802586190

Neurons and Dyspraxia (DCD)
ISBN 9781802587845

Neurons and Dyslexia
ISBN 9781802587852

Neurons and Tourette Syndrome
ISBN 9781802587838

Neurons and ADHD
ISBN 9781802587869

For more information scan the QR code:

Ariennir gan
Lywodraeth Cymru
Funded by
Welsh Government

MIX
Paper from
responsible sources
FSC® C014138